MY STEM DAY

ENGINEERING

Nancy Dickmann

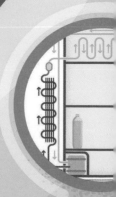

WELBECK

Published in 2021 by Welbeck Children's Books

An Imprint of Welbeck Children's Limited,
part of Welbeck Publishing Group.
20 Mortimer Street London W1T 3JW

ISBN: 978 1 78312 658 3
Printed in Dongguan, China

Design Manager: **Emily Clarke**
Editorial Manager: **Joff Brown**
Executive Editors: **Selina Wood and Nancy Dickmann**
Design: **Jake da'Costa and WildPixel Ltd.**
Picture research: **Steve Behan**
Production: **Nicola Davey**
Editorial Consultant: **Jack Challoner**

AUTHOR
Nancy Dickmann has written more than 150 non-fiction books for
children, specializing in science and history. Before becoming an
author, she worked for many years as an editor and publisher of
children's books.

STEM CONSULTANT
Jack Challoner has a degree in physics and trained as a science
and maths teacher before moving to the Education Unit at London's
Science Museum. He now writes science and technology books and
performs science shows in museums and schools.

ILLUSTRATOR
Alejandro@KJA-artists is a South American artist. He worked many
years as an art director in the advertising industry, but one day he
decided to follow his true passion and become an illustrator. Now he
creates happy images that try to put a smile on your face.

The publishers would like to thank the following sources for their kind
permission to reproduce the pictures in the book.

Page 25: (top) Busan Drone/Shutterstock, (bottom) Homo Cosmicos/
Shutterstock; 32: (right) Melinda Nagy/Shutterstock; 49: (bottom)
Mohamed Abdulraheem/Shutterstock; 56 (centre): BT Image/
Shutterstock, (bottom right): Simon Bratt/Shutterstock

Every effort has been made to acknowledge correctly and contact
the source and/or copyright holder of each picture, and Welbeck
Publishing apologises for any unintentional errors or omissions,
which will be corrected in future editions of this book.

SCIENCE TECHNOLOGY **ENGINEERING** MATHS

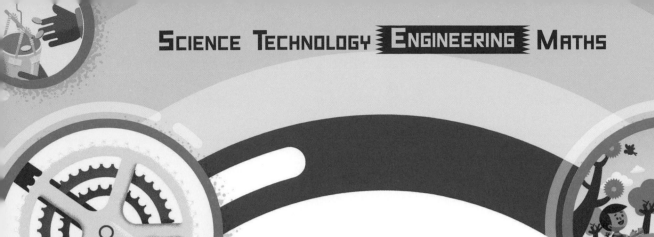

MY STEM DAY

ENGINEERING

Nancy Dickmann

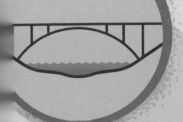

WELBECK

CONTENTS

LEARN HOW TO BUILD A BRIDGE!

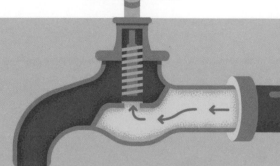

WHAT IS STEM?

STEM is everywhere in our lives. But it's not all about flowers! Instead, STEM is short for **Science**, **Technology**, **Engineering** and **Mathematics**.

Have you ever turned on a lamp, crossed a bridge or played a computer game? If so, you've already come across **STEM**. Scientists and engineers over the years have used their knowledge and skills to develop tools, structures and processes that we use every day.

Are you curious about the world around you? Do you love to ask questions and try out new ideas? Maybe you're a whizz at spotting patterns, solving problems and finding out how things work. If you try something that doesn't work out the first time, do you try again with a different approach? If so, you'll love the world of **STEM**.

Engineering is one of the four branches of STEM. It is all about using science and math to design, build and operate useful things. Engineers work in many different fields, from food production to construction, vehicle design and communication.

We use the work of engineers in our daily lives. They design our houses, build our roads and produce the plastics that we use every day. Once you know where to look, you'll spot examples of engineering everywhere you go!

THE STEM DAY TEAM

What about the rest of **STEM**? Well, **Science** investigates the natural world and all its mysteries. **Technology** is all about making useful devices and new processes. **Mathematics** is the study of numbers and shapes. These subjects work together to explore and create incredible things!

SCIENCE   TECHNOLOGY   ENGINEERING   MATH

Rise and shine!

It's time to get up

and have a shower. We take it for granted that hot water is available at the turn of a tap. But how does it work?

Most homes have a boiler that heats up water. The water is sent through pipes to radiators to heat the rooms. It also supplies the hot water taps. Many of boilers run from a main gas distribution line. The gas burns, warming up water inside the boiler. The heat energy from the gas is passed on to the water.

Some boilers can run by burning oil instead of gas. But some hot water systems are better for the planet—they use the sun's energy to heat water, instead of burning fuel. These are called solar thermal systems.

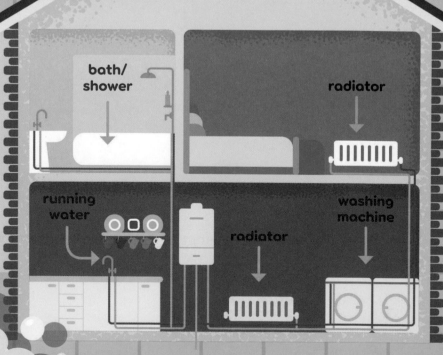

bath/shower

radiator

running water

washing machine

radiator

A solar thermal system uses panels called collectors, mounted on the roof. A black surface and a sheet of glass help to trap the sun's heat. The heat warms up water that travels through pipes inside the collector. The heated water moves through the pipes to the hot water tank. It is stored there until it is needed.

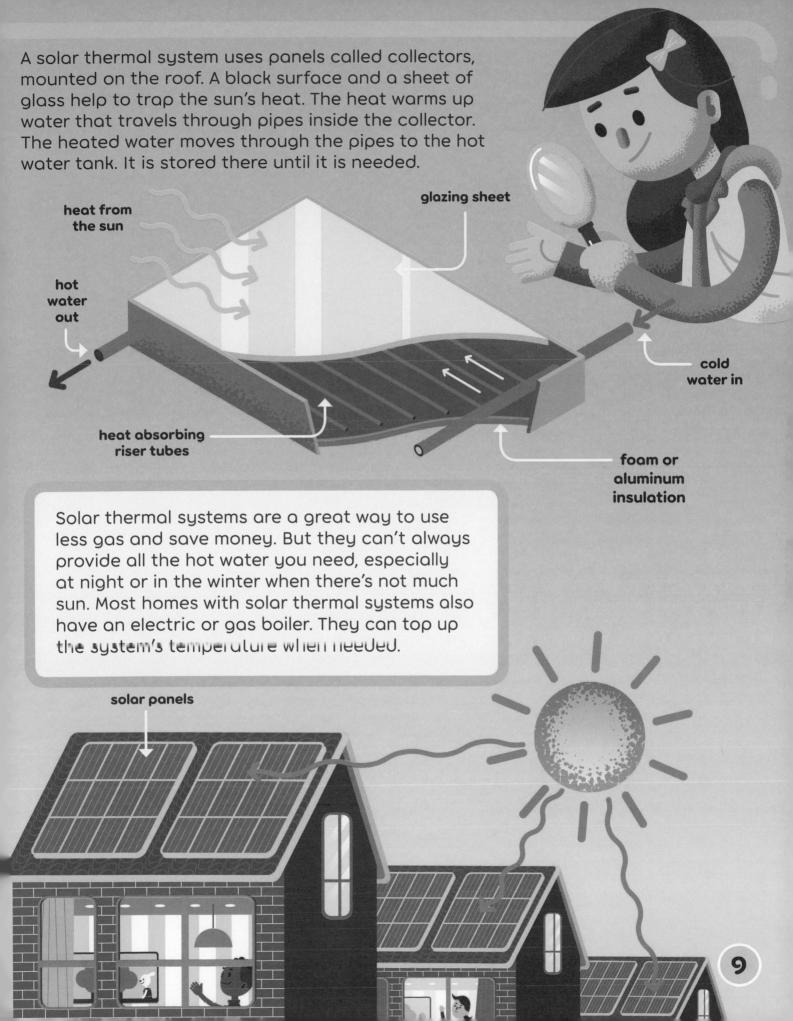

heat from the sun

glazing sheet

hot water out

cold water in

heat absorbing riser tubes

foam or aluminum insulation

Solar thermal systems are a great way to use less gas and save money. But they can't always provide all the hot water you need, especially at night or in the winter when there's not much sun. Most homes with solar thermal systems also have an electric or gas boiler. They can top up the system's temperature when needed.

solar panels

Heat water with the sun

You will need:

- 4 identical cups or glasses
- 2 sheets of white paper
- 2 sheets of black paper
- plastic wrap
- a thermometer

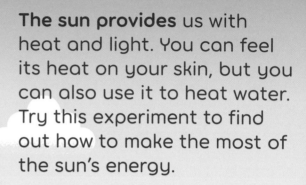

The sun provides us with heat and light. You can feel its heat on your skin, but you can also use it to heat water. Try this experiment to find out how to make the most of the sun's energy.

What to do:

1. Fill the cups with cool water from the tap. They should all have the same amount of water at the same temperature.

cool water

2. Cover two of the cups with plastic wrap.

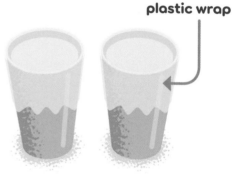

plastic wrap

3. Find a sunny windowsill or other spot, and lay out the black and white paper.

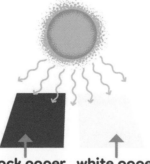

black paper   white paper

4. Put one of the cups with plastic wrap and one without on the two sheets of black paper. Do the same for the two sheets of white paper.

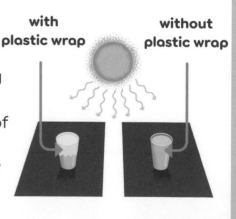

with plastic wrap   without plastic wrap

5. Leave the water to sit in the sun for at least an hour or two.

6. Use the thermometer to measure the temperature of the water in each cup.

thermometer

Which cup of water heated up the most? Dark colors absorb more heat than light colors. The plastic wrap traps heat, like the glass in a greenhouse.

Puzzle activity

Using solar power instead of natural gas to heat water saves money as well as fuel. Think about the different places in your house where you use hot water. Can you mark them on the picture?

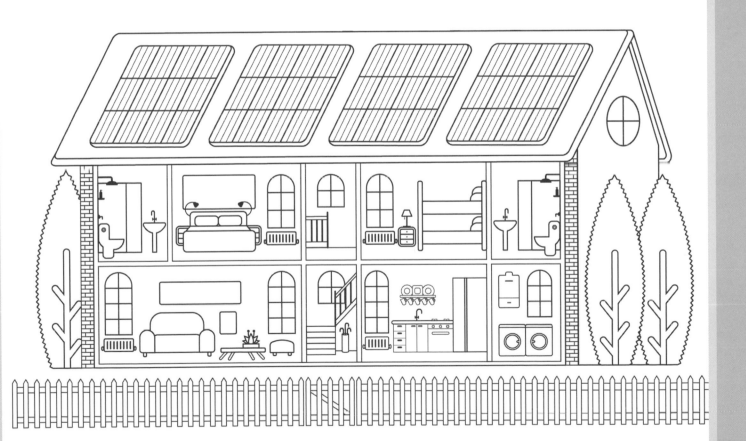

You'll find the answers at the back of the book.

A healthy smile

After breakfast, you brush your teeth. Cold, clean water flows out of the tap. But it takes a complicated system of pipes to get it there. Plumbing engineers design these systems.

A home's plumbing system is actually two separate but connected systems. One brings freshwater in, sending it to the taps, washing machine, dishwasher, and more. The other collects waste water from sinks, toilets, and showers, and takes it out of the building.

freshwater

overflow pipe

trap

air vent allows smells out

tub drain

toilet drain

waste water out

waste water

The freshwater that comes into your home is under pressure. Pressure is a pushing force, and in a plumbing system it forces water through the pipes. In some places, water is stored in a water tower. The force of gravity (the force that pulls things down to Earth) and the weight of the water forces the water through a pipe network and into homes. In other places, pumps are used to keep water under pressure.

closed tap

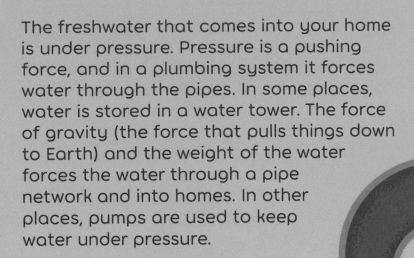

open tap

A tap is a type of valve. A valve is any mechanical device that can block a pipe (either partly or completely) to change the amount of water that flows through it. When you turn a tap on, you open the valve. This allows the pressurized water to flow out. When you turn the tap off, you close the valve.

wall

fumes

FLUSH!

vent pipe

Water in the waste water system uses gravity to travel down the pipes. Drainage pipes are all positioned downward, so gravity pulls the waste water down and out of the building.

Wacky water pressure

You will need:

- an adult to help
- an empty 2-liter bottle
- a ruler
- a marker pen
- a metal skewer
- sticky tape
- water
- outdoor space

Sharp skewer! Wet! WATCH OUT!

Gravity is one of the main ways of providing water pressure in a plumbing system. Try this simple experiment to see how it works!

What to do:

1. Use the ruler to mark out where you will make holes in your bottle. You want five holes in a straight line from top to bottom, starting about one-third of the way down the bottle. Space them evenly, about 2 inches apart.

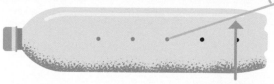

skewer

2. Ask an adult to use a metal skewer to make holes in the spots you have marked. The holes should be the same size.

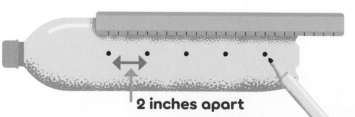

2 inches apart

3. Take a single long piece of sticky tape and cover all the holes.

sticky tape

4. Fill the bottle with water, to the top.

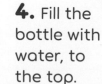

5. Take the bottle outside and quickly pull off the tape.

RRRIP!

6. Watch the way that the water flows out of the bottle. Is it the same from one hole to the next?

The bigger the weight pressing down, the higher the pressure. The water at the bottom of the bottle has more water pressing down on it than the water nearer the top. That is why the jet at the bottom is the strongest.

Puzzle activity

Pressurized water can travel up a pipe as well as down. Can you find the correct path to get water from the central supply up to the tap on the first floor?

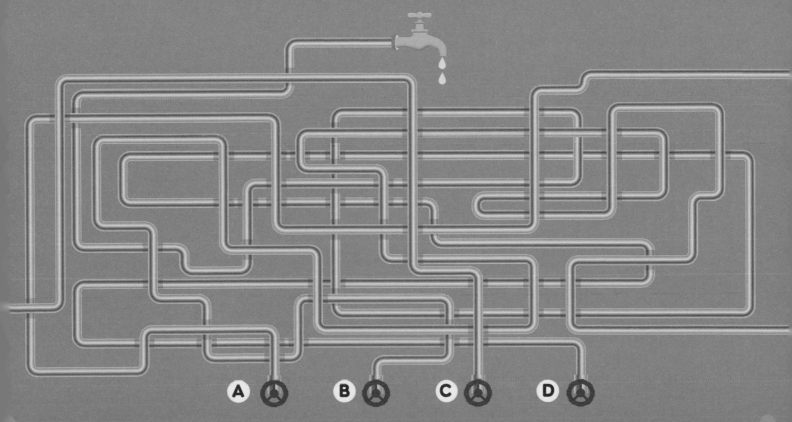

A   B   C   D

You'll find the answers at the back of the book.

On the road

WHAT A BUMPY RIDE!

How do you get to school?

Do you go by car, get the bus, or cycle? No matter how you travel, chances are that you will use an ancient bit of engineering: a road.

The earliest roads were just bumpy, muddy dirt tracks. Dragging a heavy load along one of these took a lot of effort. There was a lot of friction between the load and the ground. Friction is the force that restricts movement between surfaces sliding against each other. It slows things down.

early roads

Wheeled vehicles were invented about 6,000 years ago. They made loads easier to move. Wheels cause less friction, because they roll. There is some friction between the inside of the wheel and the axle (rod) that the wheel is connected to. Modern wheels have small parts called bearings that reduce friction even more. But wheels could get stuck in ruts and mud. When people started building smooth paved roads, wheels became even more effective.

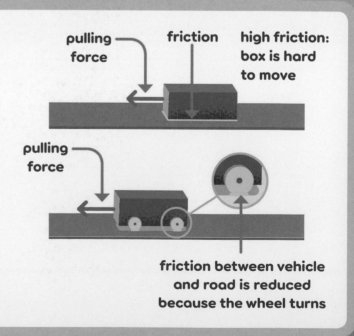

pulling force · **friction** · **high friction: box is hard to move**

pulling force

friction between vehicle and road is reduced because the wheel turns

Roman road

The ancient Romans were expert road-builders. Wherever their army went, they built roads to make it easier to move soldiers and supplies. Roman roads had a base of clay, chalk, and gravel. Large, flat stones were placed on top. They sloped slightly, so water could drain off to the sides.

bulldozer

Modern roads are still built in layers, but using heavy machinery. Bulldozers push and scrape soil to make a flat, solid base for the road. Layers of gravel are flattened by heavy rollers. The top layers of many roads are made from asphalt. This thick, sticky substance is heated, spread out, and rolled flat.

1. asphalt surface
2. base layer
3. gravel
4. compacted soil

Build your own road

You will need:

- an adult to help
- a shallow baking dish
- soft brown sugar
- a flat-bottomed glass tumbler
- rice crispies
- flat cookies
- honey
- chocolate
- a microwave-safe bowl
- a flat knife

Building roads in layers helps make them strong and stable. Layered roads are less likely to sink or crack over time. You can build your own model of a layered road out of edible ingredients!

What to do:

1. Fill the bottom of the baking dish with soft brown sugar. This represents soil. Use the bottom of the tumbler to press down on the sugar, flattening it.

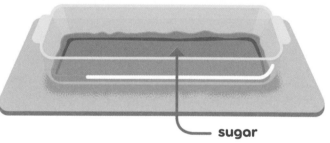

sugar

rice pops

2. Spread a layer of rice crispies over the brown sugar. This represents gravel.

3. If you want to build a Roman-style road, lay flat cookies over the top to make a road surface. These represent the stones that the Romans used.

flat biscuits

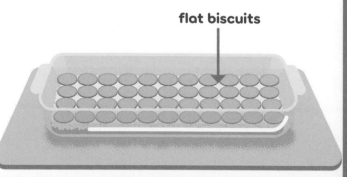

4. To make a modern asphalt road, spread honey over the rice crispies and let it settle to make a base layer. Then break the chocolate into chunks and ask an adult to help you melt it in the microwave until it's runny (check it to make sure it doesn't burn). Pour it across the honey and use a knife to spread it smooth. When it hardens, you have a road!

golden syrup   melted chocolate

Ask an adult to help.

 # Puzzle activity

Modern asphalt pavers can pave 25 feet of road in just one minute. They have a powerful engine and wheels to roll along. A hopper holds the asphalt and a conveyor belt carries it to the new road's surface. A part called the screed flattens the asphalt. Can you find five differences between these two paving machines?

You'll find the answers at the back of the book.

Stop... and go!

On your journey to school, you may need to stop at a traffic light. These electronic signals often work automatically, following a set of programmed instructions.

A simple junction where two roads cross will have at least four sets of traffic lights—one pointing in each direction on each of the two roads. All the traffic lights must work together. When one is showing green, the lights on the other road must show red. If not, there could be a serious accident!

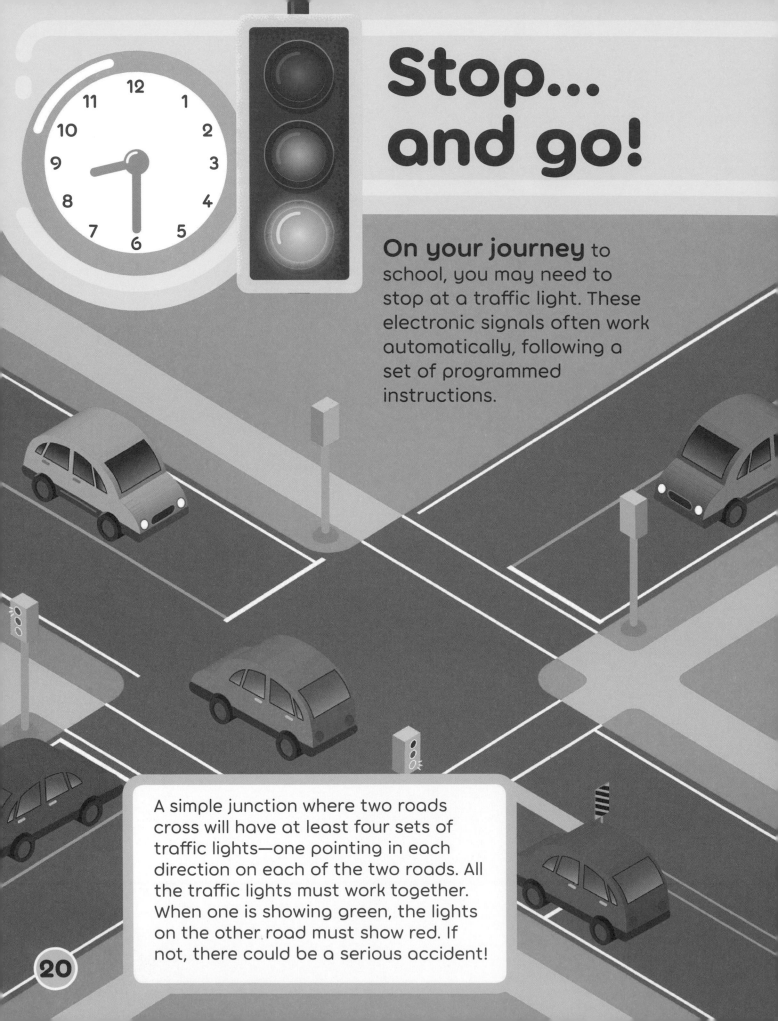

20

The simplest traffic light systems use a timer. Each light is programmed to turn green for a certain length of time, while the other lights are red. When the time is up, the light turns yellow and then red. Then the lights in the other direction can turn green. When the cycle is finished, it repeats itself over and over.

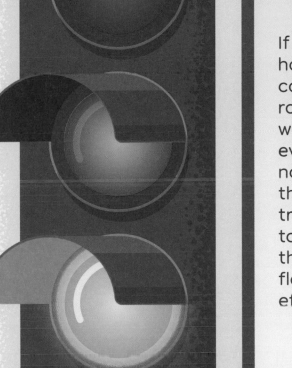

sensor

If one of the roads has very little traffic, cars on the busier road may have to wait at a red light, even if there are no cars waiting on the other road. So traffic engineers try to design systems that help traffic flow smoothly and efficiently.

Many traffic lights use lasers, cameras, or other sensors to tell how many cars are waiting. They can adjust the timing of the lights, depending on where the traffic is heaviest. Networks of these "smart" traffic lights can work together to make traffic flow smoothly across an entire city.

STOP

Program a traffic signal

You will need:

- a pencil and paper
- computer commands (see box below)

Commands:
turn red light on
turn red light off
turn amber light on
turn amber light off
turn green light on
turn green light off
wait 15 seconds
wait 10 seconds
wait 5 seconds
Repeat from beginning

Can you use the commands in the box to make a program that will let the traffic lights at this junction work together?

What to do:

1. You need to code one sequence for traffic lights 1 and 3, and a separate sequence for lights 2 and 4.

2. For traffic lights 1 and 3, you want to start on a green light. After 10 seconds, it will switch off and be replaced by the yellow light. After another 5 seconds, this switches to the red light.

3. To avoid accidents, traffic lights 2 and 4 need to show red when the other two show green. They should start on a red light that stays on for 10 seconds. Then the yellow light switches on as well. After 5 seconds of both lights showing, they switch off and are replaced by the green light.

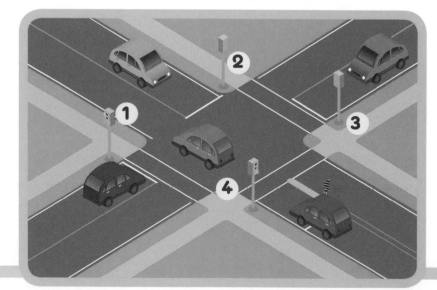

4. Draw two columns on your paper and label one "Lights 1 and 3" and the other "Lights 2 and 4".

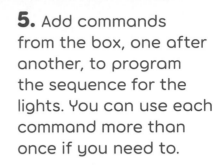

5. Add commands from the box, one after another, to program the sequence for the lights. You can use each command more than once if you need to.

 # Puzzle activity

Here is a road map of a small city. On the map, the busiest roads are wider than the less busy ones. Traffic lights are most common where busy roads cross. If you were designing a traffic light system, where would you put the lights? Draw them on the map.

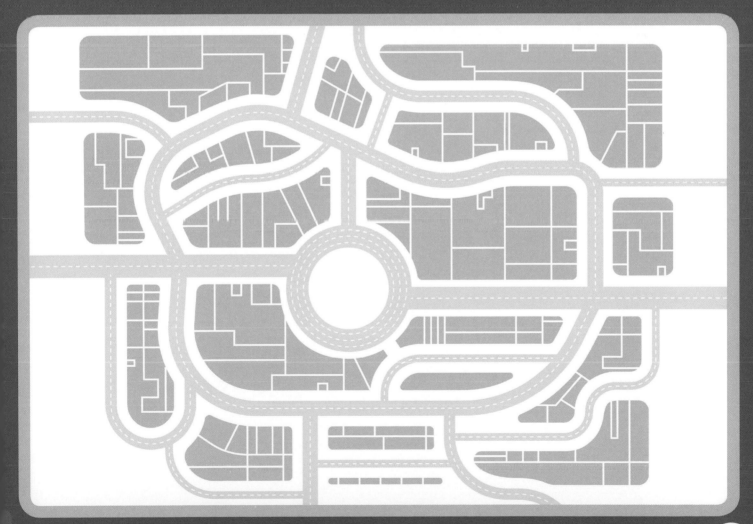

Over and under

Some roads cross each other by using a bridge or an overpass. These structures must be strong enough to carry the weight of heavy vehicles.

The earliest bridges were very simple—just a log or other long, flat object placed across a gap. This type of bridge is called a beam bridge.

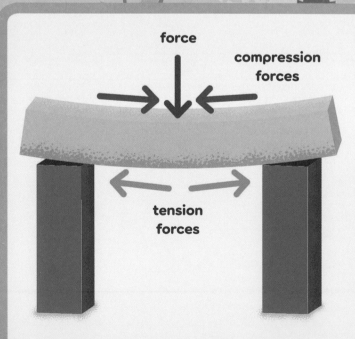

force

compression forces

tension forces

Beam bridges with longer spans have extra supports called piers. The object connecting the piers is the beam. The piers support the weight of anything crossing the beam.

Putting a heavy weight in the middle of the span puts it under stress. As the weight presses down, the top side of the beam bends in under a squashing force called compression. At the same time, the bottom side of the beam bends out under a pulling force called tension. Add enough weight, and the beam will buckle and snap.

When designing bridges, engineers think about the length of the span and the weight it must carry. Many modern road bridges are beam bridges. They are often made from concrete that is reinforced with steel. These strong materials help the beam resist compression and tension.

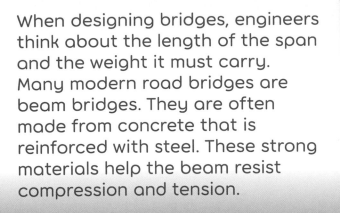

BEAM BRIDGES ARE QUICK AND EASY TO BUILD, BUT THEY ARE NOT STRONG ENOUGH TO STRETCH ACROSS LONG SPANS.

LONG BRIDGES NEED MORE ARCHES!

The ancient Romans built a different type of bridge, using arches. The weight of anything on the bridge is transferred down the arch's two strong legs. This type of design is very stable, as long as the arches aren't too big. The Romans built long bridges by using rows of smaller arches.

Build a bridge

Engineers have a lot of tricks up their sleeves to make bridges stronger. Experiment with your own bridge to see what works best!

You will need:

- several sheets of lightweight letter-sized cardboard (such as cut-up cereal boxes)
- blocks or books to use for building piers
- coins or other weights
- sticky tape
- pencil and paper

What to do:

1. Make two equal stacks of blocks or books—these are your piers. Place them close enough together so that they can be spanned by a sheet of cardboard.

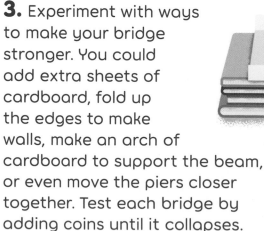

A4 card

books

coins

2. Lay a sheet of card over the top to make a bridge. Add coins until it collapses. Make a note of how many it could hold.

3. Experiment with ways to make your bridge stronger. You could add extra sheets of cardboard, fold up the edges to make walls, make an arch of cardboard to support the beam, or even move the piers closer together. Test each bridge by adding coins until it collapses.

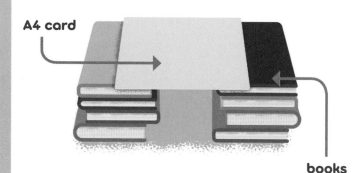

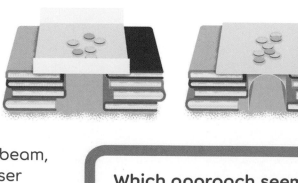

Which approach seems to work best? Can you think of any other ways to make your bridge stronger?

26

Puzzle activity

Here are some of the main types of bridges. Can you match each one to the description?

A **beam bridge** is made of a beam laid across piers.

A **truss bridge** carries traffic on a truss made of strong triangular shapes.

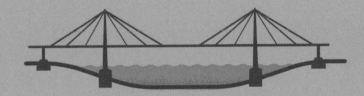

An **arch bridge** uses strong curved arches to support the weight.

A **suspension bridge** has tall towers connected by long cables. Other cables hang down from the main cables to support the deck.

A **cable-stay bridge** has towers and cables, but each cable connects directly from the tower to the deck.

You'll find the answers at the back of the book.

Super schools

You arrive at school and head for your classroom. Engineers helped to design your school, creating a building that is strong, safe and efficient.

IT ALL STARTS WITH A PLAN!

Designing a building like a school is a big job. There is more to it than just making sure there are enough classrooms, offices, and toilets. Building designers must find a way to fit in all the parts that a building needs, from stairs and walls to an electrical system.

Before construction starts, designers draw up plans for every aspect of the building.

A building's frame is the most important part. Buildings are heavy, and gravity pulls them downward. A strong frame helps to support the walls, floors, and roof. Modern buildings often have steel frames.

A FRAME IS LIKE THE SKELETON THAT HOLDS UP YOUR BODY!

Structural engineers think about gravity and other forces that act on buildings. Is the building in an area where earthquakes happen? If so, the frame must be flexible enough to shake without breaking. How much weight will each part of the building need to support? Their work keeps your school strong and stable.

Engineers must choose the right materials for every part of the building. Concrete foundations in the ground provide a hard, solid surface for the frame to rest on. Glass windows let light in, but keep heat from escaping. Special material called insulation in the walls helps to keep the building at the right temperature. Copper pipes carry water without rusting.

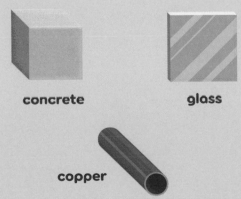

concrete

glass

copper

Terrific triangles

You will need:

- lots of old newspaper
- sticky tape
- a stapler (optional)
- a paper plate
- coins or other weights
- a friend to help

Be careful with stapler! WATCH OUT!

Structural engineers often use triangle shapes because of their strength. Make your own building and see if triangles help make it stronger.

What to do:

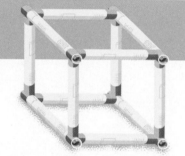

X20

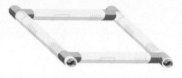

1. Roll the newspaper into tubes, each about 1 in thick and 8–10 in long. Secure them with tape. You'll need about 20 tubes.

2. Using tape or staples, connect four tubes to make a square. Then make another one just the same.

3. Attach another tube at each corner of the first square, sticking up in the same direction. Attach the second square to the top to form a cube.

4. Use six more tubes to build a second cube on top of the first.

coins   paper plate

5. Put the paper plate on top of the building and add pennies to it. How long does it take until the building collapses?

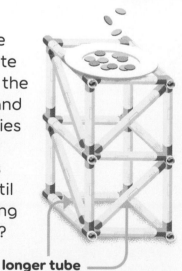

6. Roll 11 more tubes. They need to be slightly longer, so that they can stretch diagonally across the squares in your building.

longer tube

7. Attach one of these tubes as a diagonal brace across the bottom of your building.

8. Attach more tubes as braces— one in each "square" of the building, for both the bottom and top floors.

9. Put the paper plate at the top of the building again and keep adding pennies to it. How long does it take for the building to collapse now?

You will probably find that the triangular supports help to make the building more sturdy. Triangular supports are often used in real buildings.

Puzzle activity

Design your ideal house. What rooms would you include? Where would you put windows, doors, electrical wires, and plumbing pipes? Draw a floor plan as well as a view from the front. Here's an example...

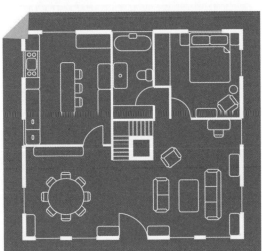

Brilliant bicycles

On a day you don't have school, you and your friends might cycle to the nearest park. Your bicycle is a simple but elegant piece of engineering!

Bicycles have a sturdy frame, two wheels, pedals, a chain, and handlebars. Within that basic design, there are many different versions. Some bicycles are best for riding over smooth roads, while others are more suited to bumpy tracks. Others are good for doing tricks. Engineers design a bicycle's parts according to what it will be used for.

Road bikes are designed for cycling along paved roads. They are built for speed, with frames made of lightweight materials. The handlebars are low, making the rider lean forward into a position that slices easily through the air. Because they are meant to be ridden on roads, they can have lightweight, skinny tires.

Mountain bikes are tough enough to stand up to rugged tracks. Their fat, treaded wheels can absorb bumps without puncturing or bending. Flat handlebars provide good steering control, and they let the rider sit up straighter to get a good view. Lots of gears make it easier to tackle hills.

WATCH THIS!

A mountain bike's front wheel is attached to a suspension fork that absorbs shocks and bumps.

BMX bikes are built for tricks. They are small, tough, and lightweight. To keep the weight down, BMX bikes often have no gears or suspension, and very simple brakes—or sometimes no brakes at all! They often have stunt pegs attached to the axles for doing tricks.

Testing gears

You will need:

- a bicycle with gears
- a pencil and paper
- a friend to help

WATCH OUT!
Keep fingers clear of gears.

A bike's gears and chain take power from the pedals to the back wheel. Connecting two gears of different sizes lets you adjust the speed at which the wheel spins.

What to do:

1. Have a look at the bicycle's gears. There are probably two or more cogs (toothed wheels) of different sizes where the pedals attach. Each has a different number of teeth around the edge. On the axle of the back wheel there will be more cogs of different sizes.

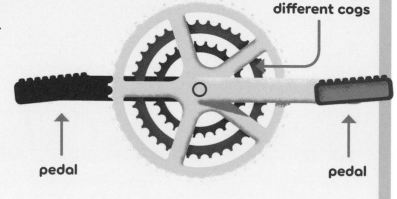

different cogs

pedal

pedal

2. Set the bike in first gear.

3. Ask your friend to help you turn the bike upside down, so that it is resting on the seat and handlebars, and the pedals and wheels can spin freely.

upside down

4. Turn the pedals five times while your friend counts how many times the back wheel spins around. (Watching the air valve going aound will make counting easier.) Make sure your friend stops counting as soon as you stop pedaling. Write down your results.

turn pedal

5. Switch the bike into second gear and then repeat steps 3 and 4.

6. Continue testing the rest of the gears and compare your results.

If a pedal cog with lots of teeth combines with a wheel cog with fewer teeth, the wheel will turn faster, but with less force. Switching to a bigger wheel cog makes the wheel spin more slowly, but with more force.

Puzzle activity

Where are these cyclists going? Follow the paths to see where each one ends up.

FINISH

Zipping along

At the playpark, you might have a go on the seesaw and queue up for the zip wire. Both rides use a combination of gravity and simple mechanics to help you have fun!

WHAT GOES UP MUST COME DOWN!

fulcrum

rigid beam

A seesaw is a type of lever. Levers have two parts: a rigid beam and a pivot point called a fulcrum. The beam balances or turns on the fulcrum. In a seesaw, the part that you sit on is the beam. The fulcrum is the middle point. When you push down on one end of the beam, the other end goes up.

Simple machines help us move or lift things. They take a force (a push or a pull) and change its direction, make it stronger, or increase the distance over which it acts. Levers and pulleys are both simple machines.

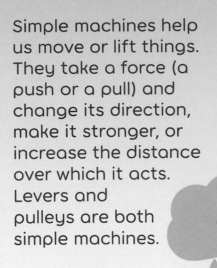

WHEEEE!

Zip wires make use of pulleys rolling along a strong steel cable. The starting point of any zip wire cable is always higher than the finishing point. This is because zip wires rely on gravity. This force pulls the rider down toward the ground, from the highest point to the lowest point.

ZZZIP!

Anything sliding down the cable will create friction. Pulleys reduce friction so you can glide faster. A pulley is a wheel with a grooved rim that the cable can fit into. The groove holds the pulley's wheel in place as it rolls down the cable. The seat of the zip wire hangs from the pulleys. You pull it up to the highest point, climb on, and let gravity do the rest!

Make your own zip wire

You don't need a pulley to build a zip wire. A smooth line and something hard and smooth to hook over it will keep friction at a minimum.

What to do:

stool or table

3–6 ft

cut →

1. Set up a line using 3–6 ft of dental floss or fishing line. Tie or stick each end to a solid object such a chair or table. One end must be higher than the other.

2. Take a straw and fold the bendy end down until it rests against the longer end. Cut it off so that you're left with a piece that has "arms" of equal length on each side of the joint. Do the same with the other straw.

3. Tape the bent straws to each side of the cup to form handles.

sticky tape

leftover straw

4. Use one of the leftover straw pieces as a bar connecting the two handles, and tape it in place.

38

paper clip

5. Bend the paper clip to form a hook that you can hook the bar over.

coins

6. Fill the cup with coins and hang it from the top end of the line.

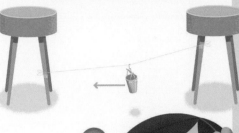

7. Let go and see how fast it moves!

You could experiment further by changing the weight or the angle of the line. Do either of these changes make the cup travel faster?

Puzzle activity

Connect the dots to see who is riding on this zip wire!

Snack time!

CHOMP!

After school you might want a snack, so you head home and open up the fridge. These appliances do a very important job: keeping food fresh.

Refrigerators use gas flowing through a system of tubes to keep the food inside cool and fresh. A tight-fitting door stops warm air from coming in.

mouldy bread

mouldy tomato

When you leave food out, bacteria and mold start to grow on it. These tiny living things can make you ill if you eat them. They grow and reproduce much more slowly when it is cold. Keeping food in the refrigerator stops them growing too quickly. This keeps food fresh longer.

RUMBLE!

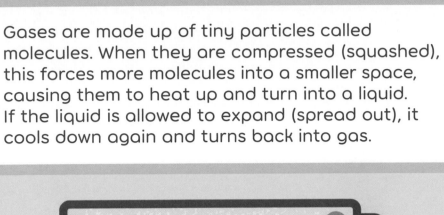

Gases are made up of tiny particles called molecules. When they are compressed (squashed), this forces more molecules into a smaller space, causing them to heat up and turn into a liquid. If the liquid is allowed to expand (spread out), it cools down again and turns back into gas.

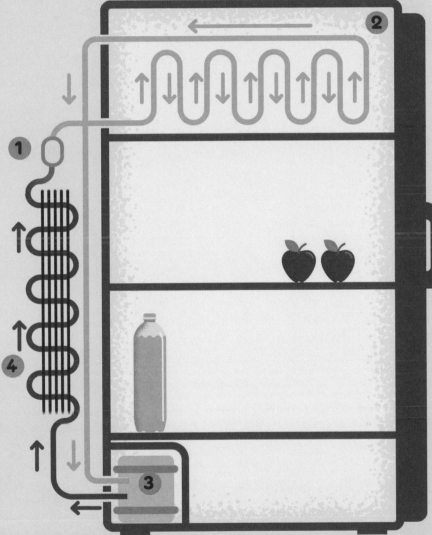

THE COOLANT CHANGES FROM GAS TO LIQUID TO GAS TO LIQUID TO GAS ...

1. Liquid coolant passes through a valve as it enters the fridge. The pressure drops and the liquid turns into a cool gas.

2. The gas in the pipe flows inside the fridge, absorbing heat.

3. As it leaves the inside cabinet, a compressor squeezes the coolant into a hot, high-pressure gas.

4. In pipes on the back of the fridge, the coolant releases some of its heat and turns back into a liquid. Then the process starts again.

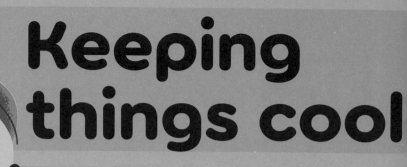

You will need:

- a terracotta plant pot big enough to fit a drink bottle inside
- another terracotta plant pot big enough to fit the other pot inside, with about 1 in clearance
- sand
- modeling clay or sticky tack
- a watering can
- a dish towel

SLURRP!

When a liquid turns into a gas it's called evaporation. When water evaporates, it cools things around it. Put this into action to cool down a drink!

What to do:

1. Use modeling clay or sticky tack to plug any holes in the bottoms of the plant pots.

sticky tack

2. Pour a layer of sand (1 in) into the larger plant pot.

sand

cold water

3. Put the smaller plant pot inside and fill the gap between the two pots with sand, all the way to the top.

fill with more sand

4. Fill the watering can with the coldest water you can. Pour it into the sand, all the way around the pot, until it is damp all the way through.

5. Wet the dish towel, wring it out and place it over the top of the pots.

wet tea towel

6. Wait an hour or two and put the drink bottle inside the pot, then cover it back up with the dish towel.

towel

7. Check your drink after another couple of hours.

As the water evaporates from the sand and the dish towel, it cools the air around it—cooling your drink as well!

TOP TIP!
STORE VEGETABLES IN THE CRISPER TO KEEP THEM FRESH FOR LONGER.

Puzzle activity

Some foods need refrigerating, others need freezing, and some—like bananas—do best out of the fridge. Draw what you like to keep in your fridge!

Helping out

After your snack, you might give your parents a hand by helping to clean the surfaces in the kitchen. Your job is made easier by soaps and cleaning sprays.

Cleaning products have different jobs. Some kill germs, some remove a chalky crust called limescale left by water, and others cut through grease. Chemical engineers design these products carefully. They use a different mixture of chemicals for each product. They must choose chemicals that are strong enough to do the job, but safe enough to use.

> MANY CLEANING PRODUCTS HAVE A MIX OF THESE THREE DIFFERENT CHEMICALS!

The chemicals in cleaning products can be divided into different categories. Solvents dissolve (mix completely with) other substances. Detergents break up and remove grease and dirt. Surfactants help a cleaning product spread out and soak into what you are cleaning. Chemicals called builders help the surfactants do this well.

Substances that can dissolve in water are given a value called pH. pH is a scale that runs from 0 to 14. Pure water is 7, right in the middle. Substances with numbers below that are called acids, and numbers above are called bases. Strong acids and bases (with very high or low numbers) can burn your skin.

lemon juice

coffee

detergent

water

soapy water

pH scale

WITH A PH OF 7, WATER IS CONSIDERED TO BE NEUTRAL. IT IS NEITHER AN ACID NOR A BASE.

Some of the chemicals in cleaning products are very strong acids or bases. They can irritate the skin. Substances with a pH closer to 7 are more gentle. Many people use natural products such as baking soda (a base) and vinegar (an acid) for cleaning. They get surfaces clean and are safer for you and the environment.

SCRUB!

Money clean up!

You will need:

- 8 old, dull pennies
- 4 glass or plastic cups
- fizzy brown soda
- water
- vinegar
- salt
- dish soap
- paper towel
- an old toothbrush (one that you can throw away afterward)
- a pencil and paper
- a plastic spoon

BLING!

Pennies start off bright and shiny but end up dark and dull. What can you use to make them shiny again?

What to do:

½ in

cola   water   salt   washing up liquid

label

1. Fill all the cups to a depth of about ½ in. One should have soda, one plain water, one vinegar with a pinch of salt stirred in, and one water with a squeeze of dish soap.

2. Write a label for each cup, so you know which is which.

3. Put two pennies into each cup and leave them to soak overnight.

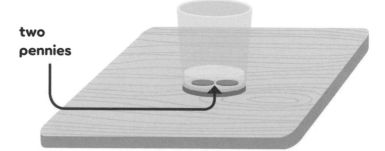

two pennies

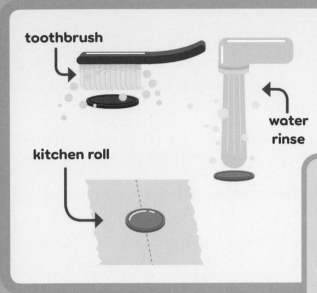

toothbrush

water rinse

kitchen roll

4. Use the spoon to scoop the pennies. Give them a scrub with the toothbrush, rinse them in water, and dry them on paper towel. Label them so that you know what they were cleaned with. Then wash your hands!

Which substance made the pennies shiniest? Most chemicals work best on certain kinds of stains. Dish soap is great on greasy dishes, but can't clean the pennies. A chemical called copper oxide makes pennies dull. It dissolves in a mixture of a weak acid (like vinegar) and salt, leaving the pennies shiny.

Puzzle activity

In most cupboards you'll find a range of different cleaning products. (Some can be dangerous, so don't handle them without an adult.) Each one in this picture has an identical partner—except one. Can you spot it?

You'll find the answers at the back of the book.

Playing with plastic

There's time for a quick play before dinner. If you look at all your toys, you'll notice that many of them are made of plastic.

When it was first invented, plastic seemed like a miracle material. It's light, strong, and can be easily colored and molded into shape. Plastics engineers have developed a huge range of different plastics. Today they are used for everything from windows and action toys to foam chair cushions.

plastic

All substances are made of tiny parts called atoms, which stick together to form molecules. Plastics are made from a kind of molecule called a polymer. Polymers are long chains of atoms—usually carbon, hydrogen, oxygen, sulfur, and nitrogen. They form repeating patterns, like a train made of many identical rail cars.

polymer molecule

BALL-AND-STICK MODELS SHOW WHAT A MOLECULE'S STRUCTURE IS LIKE.

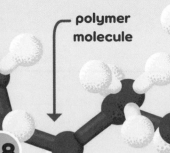

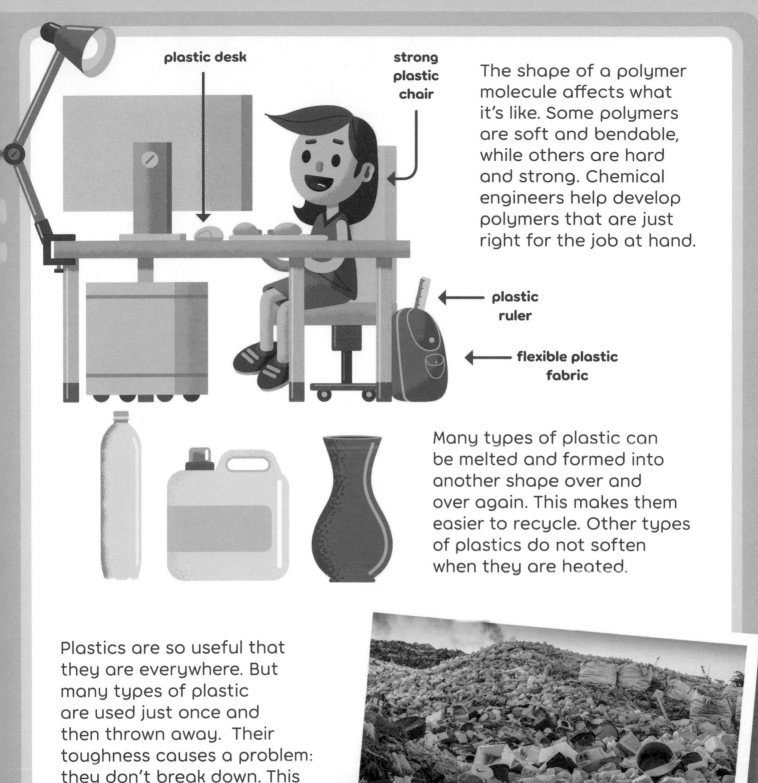

plastic desk

strong plastic chair

The shape of a polymer molecule affects what it's like. Some polymers are soft and bendable, while others are hard and strong. Chemical engineers help develop polymers that are just right for the job at hand.

plastic ruler

flexible plastic fabric

Many types of plastic can be melted and formed into another shape over and over again. This makes them easier to recycle. Other types of plastics do not soften when they are heated.

Plastics are so useful that they are everywhere. But many types of plastic are used just once and then thrown away. Their toughness causes a problem: they don't break down. This means that plastic waste is here to stay. We can help by recycling as much as possible and using less plastic in the first place.

CAN YOU FIND A NEW USE FOR ANY OF THE DISPOSABLE PLASTIC ITEMS IN YOUR HOME?

Be a plastics engineer

You will need:

- a bowl
- a spoon
- 1 cup milk
- 4 tablespoons white vinegar
- paper towel
- a sieve
- a cookie cutter

A few polymers, like rubber, are found in nature but most are created in labs and factories. You can make your own plastic in the kitchen!

What to do:

1. Pour the milk into a bowl and add the vinegar, then stir. It should start to thicken and form lumps.

stir

milk

2. After 10 minutes or so, line the sieve with a sheet of paper towel and hold it over the sink. Pour the milk and vinegar mixture into the sieve.

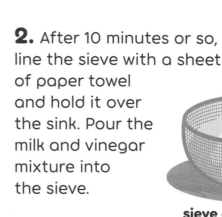

paper towel

sieve

3. It may take several minutes for the mixture to drain completely. Carefully lift out the sheet of paper towel and tip it onto more squares of paper towel.

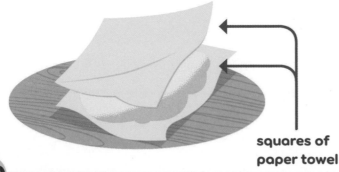

squares of paper towel

4. Press gently on your "plastic" with more paper towel to soak up any liquid. Try to get it as dry as possible.

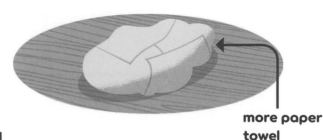

more paper towel

5. Squeeze your plastic into a ball and press it out on a countertop. When you have flattened it, press the cookie cutter into it.

squeeze

flatten

cookie cutter

6. Let the mixture sit undisturbed for at least 24 hours, until it is hard. You've made a plastic shape!

When protein molecules in the milk mix with the vinegar, they form blobs of a substance called casein. Some of the earliest plastics were made from casein.

Puzzle activity

Different types of plastics are recycled in different ways—they can't all be mixed together. Plastic items that are recyclable will have a symbol and a number. Have a look through your house for bottles, wrappers and containers that have recycling symbols, and write down an example for each number in this chart.

1 PET	
2 HDPE	
3 PVC	
4 LDPE	
5 PP	
6 PS	
7 OTHER	

Time to eat!

Do you ever give your parents a hand cooking supper? If so, you've used cooking equipment that has been designed by a materials engineer.

FLIP!

All materials have different characteristics, or properties. Some are hard and others are soft; some are see-through, while others block light. Some conduct (pass on) heat and electricity, while others don't The job of a materials engineer is to find the best material for the job, based on its properties. They often modify existing materials, or even create completely new ones.

A saucepan's main job is to heat the food inside. To do that, it needs to be made of a material that conducts heat. Metals such as aluminum and copper are good at passing on heat from the stovetop to the food inside the saucepan.

The atoms in the metal that are closest to the flame heat up first. They pass the heat energy on to the atoms above them, until the whole pan is hot.

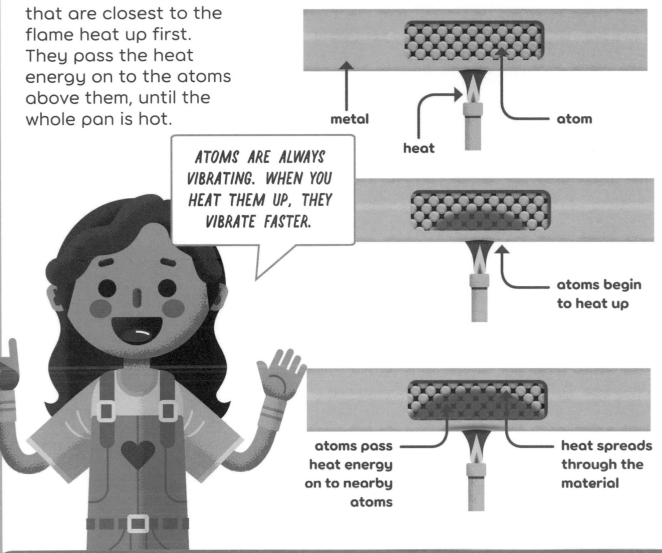

metal

heat

atom

atoms begin to heat up

atoms pass heat energy on to nearby atoms

heat spreads through the material

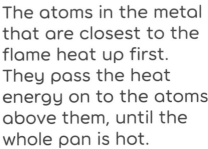

ATOMS ARE ALWAYS VIBRATING. WHEN YOU HEAT THEM UP, THEY VIBRATE FASTER.

An aluminum pan would also pass heat on to your hand if you touch it, causing a burn. The handle needs to be made of a different material—one that doesn't conduct heat well. Materials that don't conduct heat well are called insulators. Plastic and rubber are good insulators. Many saucepan handles have rubber coatings to protect your hands.

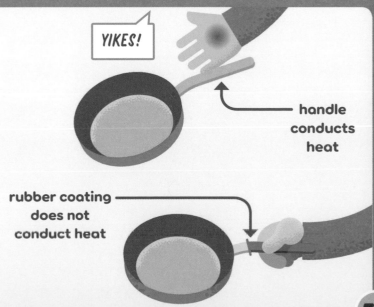

YIKES!

handle conducts heat

rubber coating does not conduct heat

Find the conductor

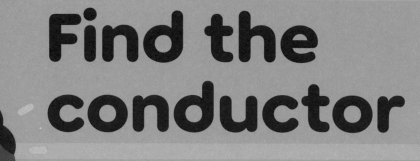

So you think you know your conductors from your insulators? Try this simple experiment to put your theories to the test.

Boiling water! WATCH OUT!

You will need:

- an adult to help
- a small glass or ceramic bowl
- 3 spoons of a similar size (one metal, one wood, one plastic)
- butter
- 3 frozen peas (or identical beads)
- a knife
- boiling water

What to do:

1. Place each spoon in the bowl, with the handle pointing down and the other end leaning over the edge.

metal   plastic   wood

2. Use the knife to put a small blob of butter at the top of each spoon.

butter

3. Stick a frozen pea or bead onto each blob of butter.

pea

4. Make sure that the spoons are all sticking out in different directions.

5. Ask an adult to carefully pour boiling water into the bowl, so the bottom 2 in of the spoon handles are covered.

boiling water

6. Watch what happens. Which pea is the first to slide down the spoon?

The different materials that the spoons are made of conduct heat at different rates. Heat moves more quickly through metal than it does through wood or plastic. The heat from the water travels quickly up the spoon, melting the butter, so the pea slides down.

Puzzle activity

All materials have different properties. Can you match each of these materials with the correct list of properties? (Make sure all three properties are a match!)

stick (wood)

t-shirt (cotton)

cling film (clear plastic)

tumbler (glass)

fork (metal)

1
- rigid (not bendy)
- rough to the touch
- does not conduct heat well

What am I? ....

2
- flexible (bendable)
- see-through
- does not absorb water

What am I? ....

3
- flexible (bendable)
- soft to the touch
- absorbs (soaks up) water

What am I? ....

4
- rigid
- see-through
- does not absorb water

What am I? ....

5
- rigid
- smooth to the touch
- conducts heat well

What am I? ....

You'll find the answers at the back of the book.

Curling up with a book

There's just time to read a chapter of your book before bed. You snuggle under the covers and press the switch on your reading lamp, then presto! Instant light.

A lamp turns on when electric current flows through it. The current flowing through the wires and the lamp is the movement of trillions of tiny particles called electrons, which move between the atoms in a substance. Like heat, it travels through some materials better than through others. Copper wire is particularly good at conducting electric current. We use electricity in a huge range of gadgets, from smartphones to kettles.

smartphone

electric kettle

Electricity can only flow through a closed loop called a circuit. If the circuit is broken, the electricity will stop flowing. In gadgets like your reading lamp, a network of wires connect with a switch, a battery, and an LED to form a circuit. An LED is a light source that glows when electricity flows through it.

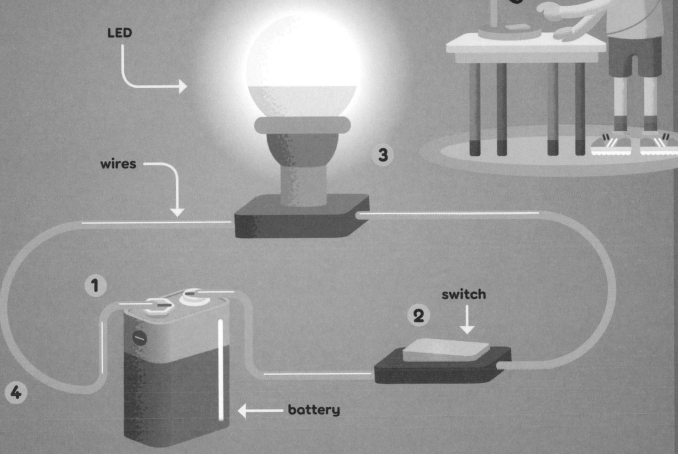

CLICK!

LED

wires

3

1

switch

2

4

battery

1. A battery stores energy in the chemicals inside it. When the battery is connected to a circuit, it can send electricity flowing around it.

2. Electricity flows from one terminal (end) of the battery through wires to the switch. If the switch is "on", the current will flow. If it is "off", the circuit is broken and no current will flow.

3. The current flows around the circuit, passing through the LED. The energy carried by the electric current lights up the LED.

4. There must be another wire connecting the LED to the other terminal of the battery. Otherwise the circuit will not be complete, and current would not be able to flow.

Fruit battery

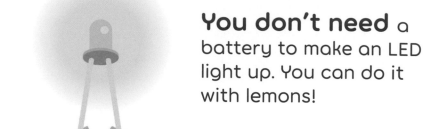

You will need:

- 4 big, juicy lemons
- 4 galvanized (zinc-coated) nails
- 4 pieces of copper wire (about 2 in long)
- 5 double-ended alligator clip cables
- low-voltage LED
- an adult to help

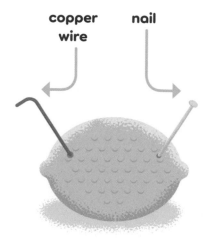

You don't need a battery to make an LED light up. You can do it with lemons!

What to do:

1. Roll the lemons on a countertop, pressing down to release the juice inside.

press and roll

2. Stick a nail into one of the lemons, near one end. Poke a piece of copper wire into the other end. Both must be deep enough to touch the juice inside, but they cannot touch each other.

copper wire   **nail**

3. Repeat step 2 with the other 3 lemons. Line them up in a row, with the nails on the right.

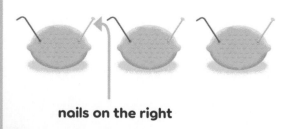

nails on the right

4. Use an alligator clip cable to connect the nail of one lemon to the copper wire of the next. Repeat until you have a "chain" of four connected lemons.

crocodile leads

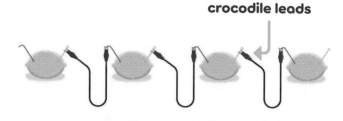

5. Attach one end of an alligator clip cable to the nail on the last lemon. Attach the other end to the negative connection on the LED (the shorter of the two wires).

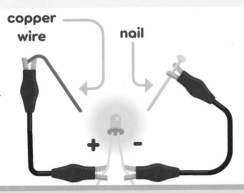
copper wire — nail
+ -

6. Attach one end of an alligator clip cable to the copper wire on the lemon at the other end. Attach the other end to the positive connection on the LED.

The LED should light up. The acid in the lemon reacts with the two different types of metal to produce a flow of electricity. One lemon isn't strong enough, which is why you connect four together. You'll need a voltage of about 3.5 for the LED to light up, so if it doesn't light you may need another lemon or two!

 # Puzzle activity

Can you find all these words to do with electricity hidden in the word search grid?

BATTERY
CIRCUIT
CONDUCTOR
COPPER
CURRENT
ELECTRICITY
ELECTRONS
ENERGY
LIGHT
SWITCH
TERMINAL
WIRES

A	U	G	T	C	K	I	F	C	L	M	B	U	C
Q	P	U	V	E	N	E	R	G	Y	F	A	S	X
O	C	N	H	T	R	L	V	D	E	M	T	I	T
E	O	T	U	B	H	E	L	P	M	I	T	B	E
S	P	V	X	Y	H	C	N	I	O	Y	E	F	R
M	P	U	D	R	X	T	V	U	Y	B	R	N	M
K	E	L	E	C	T	R	I	C	I	T	Y	H	I
Z	R	I	B	Y	R	O	V	I	D	R	M	O	N
W	B	G	F	S	W	N	G	R	M	U	P	L	A
C	G	H	B	Y	T	S	N	C	T	S	D	Z	L
P	M	T	K	F	G	E	A	U	V	W	D	U	M
J	P	Y	F	E	A	B	Y	I	W	I	R	E	S
O	G	C	U	R	R	E	N	T	Z	T	L	E	P
H	J	Y	U	V	C	P	L	A	E	C	N	H	O
C	O	N	D	U	C	T	O	R	X	H	L	G	Y

You'll find the answers at the back of the book.

Engineering everywhere!

From morning until night, our lives are made easier by engineering. Engineers use science and math to design structures and products that we use all through the day!

There are many different branches of engineering. Engineers might design spacecraft or work out what parts are needed for a food factory or plan the system of pipes that bring us fresh water.

All engineers use their knowledge of science and math to find the right materials for the job, and to make, operate and fix things. Engineers are constantly coming up with new ideas, testing them to see if they work, and learning from the results.

Engineers often work together. Projects like designing a new aeroplane or building a bridge will need the work of many different types of engineers. Do you think you might like to be an engineer one day? Think about what you've learned so far. Can you think of any problems that could be fixed with engineering? Could you design something that would help? Make sketches and plans. The sky's the limit!

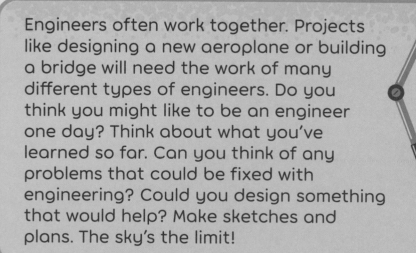

Quiz time!

Test your memory to see if you can remember the answers to these engineering questions!

1. Water flows through pipes into your home due to...

a) pressure ☐

b) solar energy ☐

c) magnetism ☐

2. What did the ancient Romans use to build roads?

a) bricks and mortar ☐

b) clay, gravel and stones ☐

c) concrete and asphalt ☐

3. Which of these tools provide a way of changing the timing of traffic lights?

a) lasers, cameras and other sensors ☐

b) remote control ☐

c) an app on a driver's phone ☐

4. The vertical structures that support a beam bridge are called...

a) cables ☐

b) trusses ☐

c) piers ☐

5. Which of these features makes mountain bikes suitable for bumpy tracks?

a) stunt pegs ☐

b) fat, knobbly wheels ☐

c) low handlebars ☐

6. Which simple machine is used in a zip wire?

a) pulley ☐

b) lever ☐

c) wedge ☐

7. What happens when a liquid evaporates?

a) it becomes thick and gloopy ☐

b) it freezes solid ☐

c) it turns into a gas ☐

8. A substance with a pH above 7 is called a...

a) solvent ☐

b) base ☐

c) surfactant ☐

Answers: 1a; 2b; 3a; 4c; 5b; 6a; 7c; 8b

61

PUZZLE ACTIVITY ANSWERS

Page 11

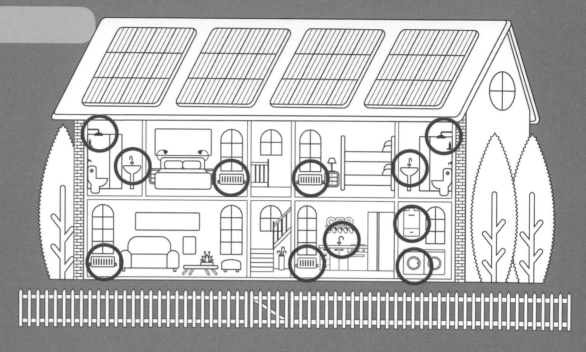

Page 15

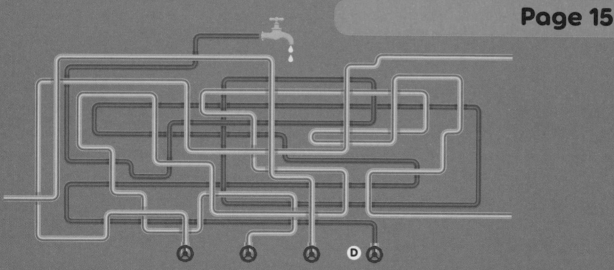

Page 19

In a real city, there would be traffic lights where the busiest roads cross, and sometimes at large roundabouts too. Is that where you put the lights on your map?

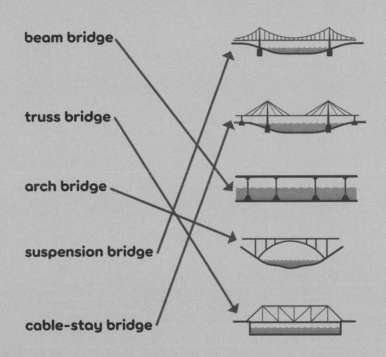

beam bridge

truss bridge

arch bridge

suspension bridge

cable-stay bridge

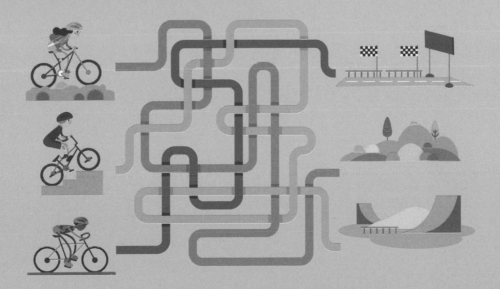

Page 39

Page 47

Page 55

1. stick (wood)
2. plastic wrap (clear plastic)
3. t-shirt (cotton)
4. tumbler (glass)
5. fork (metal)

Page 59

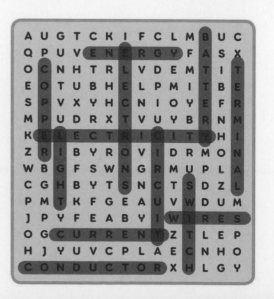